SHARING

INTIMACIES

WITH

GOD

Developing a deeper life of prayer

Pastor Emmanuel Ogbechie

Sharing Intimacies with God
Developing a deeper life of prayer
ISBN : 978-0-620-79172-4

Copyright 2018 by Pastor Emmanuel Ogbechie

Published by Divine Representatives Ministries, Inc.
P. O. Box 3631 Randburg
2125 Johannesburg, South Africa
www.diplomatsassembly.org

TABLE OF CONTENTS

INTRODUCTION

Rejoice evermore.

Pray without ceasing.

In everything give thanks: for this is the will of God in
Christ Jesus concerning you.

Quench not the Spirit.

1THESSALONIANS 5:16-19

In Paul's closing remarks in his first letter to the
Thessalonians, he gave an insightful set of
instructions all of which reveals the benefits of
praying without ceasing and sharing intimacies with
God.

He began by saying rejoice evermore. This is the
will of God for the believer in Christ.

Our Lord Jesus Christ in John 16:24 said, *"Hitherto have ye asked nothing in my name: ask, and ye shall receive, that your joy may be full."*

This reveals to us that the secret to rejoicing evermore is prayer. This was why Paul's next admonition after commanding us to rejoice is to pray without ceasing.

The cure for depression is prayer, not anti-depressants. Praying will bring you out of the pit of sadness into a domain of Joy. Are you sad? I encourage you to get up and pray!

What does it mean to pray without ceasing? It means to pray continuously and to maintain a continuous communication with God, all through every given day.

The best way to do this is through praying in tongues because the bible says that he who speaks in unknown tongues, does not speak to men but rather speaks to God in the Spirit.

When you pray in tongues, you share intimacies with God; such intimacies that gives rise to a wellspring of Joy in you.

INTRODUCTION

Joy is a product of the manifestation of the Spirit of God; and the Holy Spirit's presence manifests every time we pray.

This is the same reason why Paul admonished us not to quench the Spirit. The International standard version of that verse says, *"Do not put out the Spirit's fire."*

What is the secret to keeping the fire of the Spirit burning? It is praying without ceasing, living a Joyful and thankful life.

It is absolutely important for you to be watchful, sensitive and cautions to ensure that the fire of God's Spirit in your life does not go off.

When the fire goes off, everything about your spiritual life dies out. This is the problem with many Christians today. Many have lost the fire of the Spirit and as a result their spiritual lives have become dull and dry.

God wants you to rekindle the fire. I began to hear those words in my Spirit some time ago. The Spirit of God directed me to employ every available means to call everyone within the circle of my influence to an awakening. An awakening in prayer so we can rekindle the flames of the Spirit in our lives.

What are you waiting for? I motivate you to get into this prayer move. Pray without ceasing. You can best do this by praying in tongues.

"The one who prays using a private "prayer language" certainly gets a lot out of it," Message Translation

1CORINTHIANS 14:4a

CHAPTER 1

PRAYING ALWAYS

Pray at all times (on every occasion, in every season) in the Spirit, with all [manner of] prayer and entreaty. To that end keep alert and watch with strong purpose and perseverance, interceding in behalf of all the saints (God's consecrated people). AMP

Ephesians 6:18

The Spirit of God through the Apostle Paul gives us a divine command to pray at all times, on every occasion and in every season in the Spirit.

I would like to divinely call you to begin to devote time to prayer in obedience to this admonition of the Holy Spirit.

A continuous life of prayer is the secret to a life of continuous victory.

Paul was actually teaching on spiritual warfare when he crowned his teaching with this call to prayer as the ultimate weapon of warfare against the devil.

Most people wait until when they are under attack before they start praying; whereas by praying continuously you can stay free from any attacks.

When we pray in the Spirit always, we speak mysteries which the devil cannot comprehend. We dislodge the devil's antics and cripple his plans in such a way that they are never able to occur.

How do we pray in the Spirit? We pray in the Spirit by praying in tongues.

For he that speaketh in an unknown tongue speaketh not unto men, but unto God: for no man understandeth him; howbeit in the spirit he speaketh mysteries.

1CORINTHIANS 14:2

When you pray in tongues, no man understands you. You speak directly to God; He understands you and you are actually praying forth mysteries in the spirit realm.

PRAYING ALWAYS

God would like you to pray at all times in the spirit. In order to achieve this, you need to learn to pray in tongues all the time. In the car, while driving on the road, in your office as you work and where ever you find yourself, pray in tongues at all times.

There is an anointing about to be released upon you. There are miracles God has prepared for you. There are great and mighty things waiting to come in your direction from the realm of the Spirit. The secret to drawing from this supernatural flow is to spend time praying in tongues. I encourage you to spend time throughout today praying in tongues.

CHAPTER 2

MEN OUGHT ALWAYS TO PRAY

And he spake a parable unto them to this end, that men
ought always to pray, and not to faint;

Luke 18:1

The Holy Spirit would like us to pay attention to the
subject of Prayer and dedicate ourselves afresh to
spending time In His Presence daily.

God wants to usher us into a new dimension of His
anointing. The first initial outpouring of the Holy
Spirit came when the early Apostles stayed in the
upper room in prayer for several days.

Our Lord Jesus Christ before he left actually
commanded us to tarry in His presence in prayer

until we are clothed with His divine power from on high.

I want to motivate you to rise up in the place of prayer. Men ought always to pray. God wants us talking to Him regularly throughout every given day. This is why the first evidence of being filled with the Holy Spirit is speaking in tongues.

When we speak in tongues, we do not speak to men but rather we speak to God. Praying in tongues all the time is the secret to praying always.

Our Lord Jesus Christ Himself prayed always. Beginning from when He was being water baptised, He practised praying always. While everyone was just waiting to be dipped into the water by John, the scripture records that He was in prayer and it led to the outpouring of the Holy Spirit.

I love the way the amplified translation renders Luke 18:1

ALSO [Jesus] told them a parable to the effect that they ought always to pray and not to turn coward (faint, lose heart, and give up).

Men ought always to pray and not to turn cowards in the face of the devil's threats. Prayerlessness will make you become a coward and unable to stand up against the wiles of the devil.

Cowardly people run when no one is pursuing them but righteous, prayerful people are usually bold like a lion.

The prophet Isaiah said in Isaiah 40:31 that those who wait for the Lord, those who seek Him in prayer and put their hope in Him; they shall change and renew their strength and power; Alleluia.

Those who pray always, they shall lift their wings and mount up [close to God] as eagles [mount up to the sun]; they shall run and not be weary, they shall walk and not faint or become tired.

I encourage you today to separate yourself from distractions. Cleanse yourself from everything that contaminates your spiritual walk and draw nigh to God in prayer. When you do, His presence will pour all over you in a manifest way like rain from heaven.

I pray that the spirit of prayer will rest upon you now and that the Holy Spirit will draw you into deep times of praying in Jesus name

CHAPTER 3

BUILD YOUR SPIRITUAL HOUSE

Go up to the mountain, and bring wood, and build the
house; and I will take pleasure in it, and I will be
glorified, saith the LORD.

Haggai 1:8

Go up to the mountain and build up your life as a
spiritual house unto the Lord, so that He can take
pleasure in it.

Did you know that going up to the mountain means
taking time out of your busy schedules to get into
prayer?

Did you know that you are God's house today that needs to be built up?

Did you know that part of the spiritual wood that builds up your life refers to the utterance which the Holy Spirit gives to you when you pray in tongues?

Jude verse 20 declares; *"But ye, beloved, building up yourselves on your most holy faith, praying in the Holy Ghost,"*

You build up yourself a spiritual house unto God when you pray in the Holy Ghost. You pray in the Holy Ghost by praying in tongues.

God is not pleased with the spiritual state of many Christians. The spiritual house of most believers is in shambles because of prayerlessness.

Haggai wrote this prophecy many years ago;

Thus speaketh the LORD of hosts, saying, This people ,say, The time is not come, the time that the LORD'S house should be built.

Then came the word of the LORD by Haggai the prophet, saying,

Is it time for you, O ye, to dwell in your ceiled houses, and this house lie waste?

BUILD YOUR SPIRITUAL HOUSE

HAGGAI 1:2

When you do not dedicate time to God in prayer like you ought, you are actually saying by such action that it is not time for God's house to be built.

Imagine that you live in a house that has proper ceiling whereas you expect God to come live in a house that is not properly built!

Verse 7 of Haggai 1 warns us to consider our ways and get into the task of building up ourselves on our most holy faith, praying in the Holy Ghost.

Do you sometimes wonder why it seems like God does not take pleasure in you? God wants to take pleasure in you; but the challenge is that your spiritual life is not built up so you cannot connect with God the way He wants to do with you.

You need to go up to the mountain of prayer and give yourself to praying in tongues and thereby build up yourself on your most holy faith, praying in the Holy Ghost.

God said, when you begin to pray like you ought to, He will take pleasure in you and beautify your life with His glory.

Prayer is what brings the glory of God into manifestation in the temple. Our bodies are the temples of the living God. God's glory is supposed to be upon your life every day; the secret to enjoying this divine presence is praying always with all prayer and supplication in the Spirit.

I motivate you today to begin to pray in tongues and build up yourself so God can come and dwell in your life in a manifest way.

Prayer: "Father draw me, and I will run after you. Quicken me in the place of prayer and I will call upon thy name. Bring me into your chambers and I will rejoice and be glad in thee"

CHAPTER 4

THE EFFECTS OF PRAYING IN THE SPIRIT

And it came to pass about an eight days after these sayings, he took Peter and John and James, and went up into a mountain to pray.

And as he prayed, the fashion of his countenance was altered, and his raiment was white and glistering

Luke 9:28-29

There are amazing benefits of praying in the spirit which God wants us to tap into.

In this account our Lord Jesus Christ went up into a mountain to pray and took some of His disciples with Him to teach them how to pray.

It is important for leaders to lead by example in communicating the art of praying. It is also important if you will catch the spirit of prayer to associate with people who pray.

If most of your friends are prayerless you will be prayerless yourself.

The experience of praying sometimes can be likened to climbing a physical mountain. Initially it seems difficult but as you persist and continue you end up succeeding at it.

As our Lord Jesus prayed, the scripture recorded that the fashion of his countenance was altered. This is an amazing effect of prayer.

Every time you spend time in prayer, something changes in you.

The Amplified translation renders that verse this way: *"As He was praying, the appearance of His face became different [actually transformed], and His clothing became white and flashing with the brilliance of lightning."*

When you pray the appearance of your face changes; depression leaves you, sadness and its root causes are driven away.

Jesus' clothes became white and glistering with the glory of the father. Similarly, everything associated with you becomes affected positively. When you pray even your wallet becomes blessed through prayer.

If you are going through a depressing situation, you need to get up and start praying in the spirit. Praying in the spirit means praying in tongues.

Verse 30 of the same book of Luke chapter 9 reveals to us that while our Lord Jesus was praying two men appeared to Him in glory and revealed things to Him to prepare Him for His future.

Praying in the spirit connects you to the glory realm. I motivate you to begin to pray in the spirit always. When you are in the spirit you will begin to see revelations yourself.

Why it is that many Christians are being deceived by people who are operating with familiar spirits and demons today? It is because they want to see revelations.

God is showing you here a pattern. If you want to see revelations and you want to encounter God's glory, then get into prayer. Pray in tongues until the doors of heaven are opened to you and a voice from the excellent glory calls out to you.

Stop running around looking for prophets to tell you your future. Start praying in tongues and the Holy Spirit will show you great and mighty things.

CHAPTER 5

ADVENTURES IN PRAYER

And when they had prayed, the place was shaken
where they were assembled together; and they were
all filled with the Holy Ghost, and they spake the
word of God with boldness.

ACTS 4:31

The bible chronicles accounts of men and women
who devoted time to prayer and shows us how their
prayer adventures brought about an outpouring of
the Holy Spirit.

Many years ago when the Lord began to deal with
me about prayer, my heart became so overwhelmed
with a desire to obey Him that it drove me into

places and times of praying that when I look back today I could not have imagined what took me into those places.

I had a friend who shared the same passion as I did. One day we jointly went into a school at night when every place was dark and prayed all night .

While we were praying in the thick darkness (as there was no electricity in the school hall), a security guard who worked in the school came into the dark hall with his touch light and screamed out to us saying, 'Who are those there?' Then we responded by saying we are the ones and we are praying.

The man could not believe that young boys of about the age of 16 and 18 years would be all alone in a dark school hall where no one else was without electricity but in absolute thick darkness praying.

So was our hunger. God wants us to be so hungry for His presence that it will cause us to find quiet places where we can devote time to Him in prayers.

In those days, my Dad was pastoring an Anglican Church, when it was night and everyone was getting ready to sleep, I would request for the key to his church and go there at night alone and pray.

The more I sought the Lord the more I wanted more of Him.

At those times there was no social media like we have today. All we had was the bible and consecration to prayer was like going on facebook to browse.

God wants us to prioritize His presence and separate time for prayer.

There is a praying that we must return to in this generation if we will see a mighty manifestation of the Holy Spirit in our days.

God promised in Haggai 2:6 to shake nations and to cause the desires of all nations to come. This shaking will come when we begin to spend quality time in prayers seeking the outpouring of the Holy Spirit.

Some years ago, a friend of mine spent the whole day in prayer, praying in tongues. In the evening of that day, his fiancée came to see him and saw his face all white. So she thought he had put some powder on his face and she tried to wipe the powder off.

The moment she touched his face she screamed because the glory of God went through her hands and electrified her whole body.

She later discover that what she thought was white powder on his face was actually the glory of God pouring out of his face after spending a whole day in prayer.

The scripture declares that Moses wist not that the skin of his face did shine as God talked with him.

I encourage you to give yourself to praying in tongues deeply

CHAPTER 6

WHEN THEY HAD PRAYED

And when they had prayed, the place was shaken where they were assembled together; and they were all filled with the Holy Ghost, and they spake the word of God with boldness.

ACTS 4:31

There are amazing benefits of praying. When we pray, supernatural things start happening. After the Apostles had prayed the place where they were was shaken and they were all filled with the Holy Ghost.

What did these Apostles pray for and why is it that many times we do not see these types of results which the Apostles had in their days?

The simple answer is that the Apostles prayed for the manifestation of the Holy Spirit and for boldness in preaching the word of God; both of which are in line with God's will.

When we pray in line with God's will, we will definitely receive answers to our prayers. The number one will of God for your life as a Christian is that God wants you to be continuously filled with His Holy Spirit.

Think about it, when last did you devote time to prayer solely to request a fresh infilling with the Holy Spirit? I am sure most people can remember when last they prayed for other things other than just being in prayer asking for a fresh infilling with the Holy Spirit.

Wherefore be ye not unwise, but understanding what the will of the Lord *is*.
And be not drunk with wine, wherein is excess; but be filled with the Spirit;

Ephesians 5:17-18

In Ephesians 5:17 Paul admonished us not to be unwise but to know what the will of God for our lives is. It is unwise for you to focus your pursuits on the things of this life rather than pursuing God's will for your life. In verse 18 Paul revealed that the will of God is for you to be continuously filled with the Holy Spirit.

I love the way the message translation renders Ephesians 5:18 it says *"Drink the Spirit of God, huge draughts of Him"*

Amplified translation says, *"Ever be filled and stimulated with the Holy Spirit"*

I motivate you to seek a continuous infilling with the Holy Spirit and the way to do this is by you devoting time to prayer primarily to ask for an infilling with the Holy Spirit.

The Apostles prayed corporately about this and there is a lot of benefit when a group of people come together just to seek the fire of the Holy Spirit in corporate prayer. Many Christians do not know how important it is to attend corporate prayer meetings when their local church calls for it. As a result they miss out from this shaking of the Holy Ghost that transforms lives.

Praying brings a shaking into things that needs to be shaken. God promised in Haggai that He would shake things. This shaking comes when the power of the Holy Spirit begins to fill your life afresh.

I pray that the Holy Spirit will fall upon your life afresh and everything that ought not to be there will be shaken out in Jesus mighty name.

Rise up and pray!

CHAPTER 7

COME UP TO THE LORD

And the LORD said unto Moses, Come up to me into the
mount, and be there: and I will give thee tables of stone,
and a law, and commandments which I have written;
that thou mayest teach them.

EXODUS 24:12

There is no greater call than to be invited by God
into His presence. God invited Moses to come up
into the mountain and be there for some days.

This scripture means little or nothing to Moses
today because Moses is dead and gone; rather this
scripture is God's injunction to every serious
believer.

God is saying, *'come up to me into the mountain.'* Going up to God in the mountain for Moses implied that he had to separate himself from activities and busy schedules and from the crowd to be in God's presence in prayer.

Many believers have lost the fire and glory of God because of activities and busy schedules. God is calling you apart; He is saying come up to the mountain.

Many times when Jesus went up to the mountain, He went there to pray. Prayer has always been the way to connecting to God in a deeper way. Praying with fasting amplifies God's presence and power in your life.

God said to Moses, if you come up to me I will give thee tables of stone, a law or principles of life which will separate Israel from all other nations and make them a unique people.

God has things ready to deliver into our hands in this generation. There is a glory waiting to manifest but we must first come up to Him into the mountain by spending time in prayer.

COME UP TO THE LORD

God never planned for His Children to struggle like the world, His plan is for us to live by revelations of His principles for victory. These principles reside with the Holy Spirit today but He is waiting for you to come up into the mountain of prayer, in communion and fellowship with Him.

Spending time in prayer can be likened to climbing a mountain. When going up into a mountain, the force of gravity will generally try to pull you down. However to get to the top you have to persist.

When you begin to devote time to prayer, you will face several obstacles. Distractions of different kinds; the devil will try hard to stop you from spending time in prayer. I encourage you not to allow those distractions hinder you. Persistence is important if you will attain unto a new height with God.

God is calling you today like He called Moses, He says, *'Come up to the mountain and be there!'* Get rid of distractions today, withdraw yourself and devote time to prayer.

I like the part that says *'...and be there';*

This implies tarrying in God's presence. Not being in a hurry to leave the place of prayer. Most times when we go to prayer, we are always so time conscious that we leave God's presence before God finishes dealing with us.

When Moses went up to the mountain, he had no time frame of how long he would spend there.

The scripture records in Exodus 32:7 that God literarily drove him out of his presence after forty days so he could go and attend to the children of Israel who had backslidden and made a golden calf to lead them back to Egypt because they thought that Moses was never going to come back.

God wants us to learn to tarry in His presence until He instructs us to leave to go attend to other things.

I pray for grace to withdraw from all distractions of this age so you can begin to spend time in God's presence in Jesus name.

CHAPTER 8

POWER THROUGH PRAYER

And the prayer of faith shall save the sick, and the Lord shall raise him up; and if he have committed sins, they shall be forgiven him.

Confess your faults one to another, and pray one for another, that ye may be healed. The effectual fervent prayer of a righteous man availeth much.

Elias was a man subject to like passions as we are, and he prayed earnestly that it might not rain: and it rained not on the earth by the space of three years and six months.

And he prayed again, and the heaven gave rain, and the earth brought forth her fruit.

JAMES 5:15-18

Tremendous spiritual power is released when righteous men who know that they are the righteousness of God pray.

Elijah demonstrated that though we are surrounded by physical challenges we can gainfully employ the power of prayer to cause changes. Elijah was a man of like passions or physical challenges as we are, yet he prayed earnestly and his prayer stopped rain from falling for 3 and 1/2 years.

The power of prayer is an untapped reservoir of spiritual energy which is available to every believer.

When you spend time praying, it is important for you to be aware that you are actually putting forth spiritual energy that is dynamic in its workings.

The Amplified Translation renders the later part of James 5:16 thus: *"The earnest (heartfelt, continued) prayer of a righteous man makes tremendous power available [dynamic in its working]."*

Prayer makes tremendous power available. Continued praying makes power continuously available that is dynamic in its working.

POWER THROUGH PRAYER

This is what our Lord Jesus Christ meant when He instructed the disciples to tarry until they are endued with Power from on high in Luke 24:49.

To tarry speaks about spending protracted times in prayer.

Elijah used this prayer principle in his days. He prayed and shut the heavens and he prayed again and the heavens gave rain.

God has given us the art of praying as a tool to elevating ourselves beyond the limits of the earthly limitations we may find ourselves in.

I encourage you today to begin to engage in prayer, especially praying in tongues.

Praying in tongues causes the river of the Holy Spirit that dwells within your human spirit to begin to be pumped out into your physical body where it can be useable.

This is why everyone needs to receive the gift of praying in tongues.

You will discover that when you pray in tongues for a long period of time, your physical body becomes electro static and is charged up with God's divine power in such a way that it begins to conduct God's power.

You have a lot of time you can use in praying in tongues, so I encourage you to start today.

Do not wait for a special retreat before you start praying. Pray on the go! Pray in tongues while you drive. While you cook, while working on your desk at work, pray in tongues. You can literarily pray in tongues all day that way.

CHAPTER 9

SHARING INTIMACIES WITH GOD

And these signs shall follow them that believe; In my name shall they cast out devils; they shall speak with new tongues;

MARK 16:17

Why should you pray in tongues all the time?

Our Lord Jesus said that speaking in tongues will be a sign that will follow those who believe on Him.

Do you believe on the Lord Jesus Christ? If the answer is yes, then you need to know that speaking in tongues, is one of the signs that must follow you as evidence that you believe on Jesus.

For he that speaketh in an unknown tongue speaketh not unto men, but unto God: for no man understandeth him; howbeit in the spirit he speaketh mysteries.

1CORINTHIANS 14:2

An important reason why you should pray in tongues all the time is because He who speaks in tongues does not speak to men but rather He speaks unto God.

Wouldn't you like to speak to God all the time? God has provided you with the gift of speaking in tongues so that you can talk to Him privately in heaven's intimate dialect.

Should everybody speak in tongues?

The answer is yes. Everybody should be able to speak to God privately. However, as a result of lack of proper knowledge on this subject, many people do not do so.

"If you praise him in the private language of tongues, God understands you but no one else does, **for you are sharing intimacies just between you and him.**" Message Translation

1CORINTHIANS 14:3

When we pray in tongues we are actually praising God in a private language. God understands us but no one else does.

You should never worry about not understanding what you are saying in tongues because according to this scripture, only God understands.

When you pray in tongues you are actually sharing intimacies with God, just between you and Him.

This is why God wants you to pray in tongues all the time.

God wants you praying while you work, while you cook, while you drive and so on. You can literarily pray continuously in tongues all day long.

When you pray in tongues always, you share intimacies with God. Wouldn't you like to be intimate with God all day long?

I admonish you to devote yourself to this.

If you have not yet received the gift of the Holy Spirit with the evidence of speaking in tongues, you really are missing out on a level of intimacy which the gift of tongues enables you to share with God.

Do not let the devil or anyone deceive you into thinking that not everybody should speak in tongues.

Jesus said speaking in tongues was a sign that will follow all believers so why should you be the odd man out?

Many Christians are suffering from spiritual dryness today because they are not taking advantage of this amazing gift of the Holy Spirit.

You cannot be intimate with God and feel spiritually dry.

You develop intimacy with God when you pray in tongues. I invite you to allow this river begin to flow out of your belly endlessly.

CHAPTER 10

THE FATHER IS SEEKING FOR SPIRIT WORSHIPPERS

But the hour cometh, and now is, when the true worshippers shall worship the Father in spirit and in truth: for the Father seeketh such to worship him.

God is a Spirit: and they that worship him must worship him in spirit and in truth.

JOHN 4:23-24

Our Lord Jesus Christ prophesied about a coming hour; the time and season when men will pray and worship God the father in the Spirit.

The dispensation of praying and worshipping in tongues is only unique to the Church age after the giving of the Holy Spirit.

God is a Spirit: and those who worship Him must worship Him in Spirit and in truth.

The secret to worshipping God in Spirit is found in 1Corinthians 14 :2

For he that speaketh in an unknown tongue speaketh not unto men, but unto God: for no man understandeth him; *howbeit in the spirit* he speaketh mysteries.

Notice that it says when you speak in tongues, **"you speak to God in the Spirit."**

"If you praise him in the private language of tongues, God understands you but no one else does, for you are sharing intimacies just between you and him." Message Translation

When you pray in tongues, you actually are praising and worshipping God in the Spirit. You share intimacies just between you and Him.

The father is seeking for true worshippers. The father is seeking for Spirit Worship. He is tired of

carnal, unpassionate dry worship. The father wants us to get in the Spirit, we do this by praying in tongues.

This is so important to God our father as a result every time when God fills any believer with His Holy Spirit, the first gift He gives to them is the gift of speaking in tongues.

When the Holy Spirit fell upon the disciples, the first thing they did was that they spoke in tongues because the father wants Spirit worship. Spirit worship is done through praying in tongues.

When the Holy Spirit gave interpretation to the words which the Apostles where speaking in tongues on the day of Pentecost, the people who heard them were amazed at the kind of worship and praise which only the Holy Spirit can inspire.

For they said in Acts 2:11b *"we do hear them speak in our tongues the wonderful works of God."*

The Apostles praised the wonderful works of God by speaking in tongues.

At Cornelius' house when the Holy Spirit came upon the people, the first gift He gave them was the gift of speaking in tongues. He did so because the father's ultimate desire is Spirit worship and Spirit praise.

We become Spirit worshippers when we worship and pray in tongues a lot. The people who went with Peter to Cornelius' house were also amazed like the strangers in Acts 2 when they heard the Gentiles speak in tongues and magnify God.

For they heard them speak with tongues, and magnify God. Then answered Peter,

ACTS 10:46

When we speak in tongues we magnify God in the spirit.

God is seeking for people to worship Him in tongues. I encourage you to engage in it without ceasing.

Pray in tongues until you feel the glory falling around you.

CHAPTER 11

HOW TO RECEIVE THE GIFT OF SPEAKING IN TONGUES

Receiving the Holy Spirit with the evidence of speaking in tongues is a very simple process if you pay attention to the following.

Firstly you need to know that the Holy Spirit is a gift. Just like every other gift, He comes to you freely. You do not work to receive Him. He actually wants to fill your life more than you may want to receive Him.

Secondly, **the gift of speaking in tongues is the result of being filled with the Holy Spirit** as can be seen from the following scriptures.

And they were all filled with the Holy Ghost, and began to speak with other tongues, as the Spirit gave them utterance.

ACTS 2:4

While Peter yet spake these words, the Holy Ghost fell on all them which heard the word.

And they of the circumcision which believed were astonished, as many as came with Peter, because that on the Gentiles also was poured out the gift of the Holy Ghost.

For they heard them speak with tongues, and magnify God.

ACTS 10:44-46

And when Paul had laid his hands upon them, the Holy Ghost came on them; and they spake with tongues, and prophesied.

ACTS 19:6

We see from all these scriptures that speaking in tongues is the result of being filled with the Holy Spirit.

Are you qualified to receive the Holy Spirit?

HOW TO RECEIVE THE GIFT OF SPEAKING IN TONGUES

The answer is yes. God does not give the Holy Spirit based on your works or self-righteousness. He gives Him as a free gift and all you need is to receive it by faith.

And these signs shall follow them that believe; In my name shall they cast out devils; they shall speak with new tongues;

Mark 16:17

Our Lord Jesus here in Mark 16:17 said, that everyone who believes on Him will be able to speak with new tongues. The only question you need to ask yourself is, do I believe in Jesus? If the answer is yes then you qualify to receive.

Some people believe that not everybody can receive the gift of speaking in tongues because of 1 Corinthians 12:30 which says, *"Have all the gifts of healing? do all speak with tongues? do all interpret?"*

Firstly, you must know that not everyone speaks in tongues; not because every cannot receive it but because not everyone is knowledgeable about it. What you do not know about you cannot take advantage of.

Also it is important to note that the gift of speaking in tongues operates in two ways.

The first operation is when it is used as a ministry tool to minister to people while the second operation is when it is used as a prayer language to speak only to God.

The first operation is given as the Holy Spirit wills depending on the assignment He has for you primarily to minister to people. Not everyone can operate in this.

The second operation is a prayer use and every Christian is expected to have it because every Christian is supposed to be able to speak to God privately in prayer according to the following meeting;

For he that speaketh in an unknown tongue speaketh not unto men, but unto God: for no man understandeth him; howbeit in the spirit he speaketh mysteries.

1CORINTHIANS 14:2

To receive the gift of the Holy Spirit all you need to do is just ask for it, and after asking, believe that you have received and you shall have.

HOW TO RECEIVE THE GIFT OF SPEAKING IN TONGUES

When the Holy Spirit comes upon you, He comes into you with the gift of speaking in tongues. You must begin to speak in tongues as the Holy Spirit gives you the utterance.

Please note that the Holy Spirit does not speak in tongues, we are the ones who speak. The Holy Spirit simply gives you utterance of what to say, and then you have to speak forth what He puts in your spirit.

Also note that you do not learn or copy somebodies tongues. Your tongue does not have to sound sweet or nice either. You must believe that it is the Holy Spirit giving you the words and then you must speak them forth in faith.

The devil will try to discourage you from speaking in tongues by telling you that you are forming it. He may even tell you that your tongue does not sound sweet or that you do not understand what you are saying, all in an attempt to stop you. You must refuse to listen to him.

When you speak in tongues, you will naturally not understand what you are saying but God understands.

SHARING INTIMACIES WITH GOD

For he that speaketh in an unknown tongue speaketh not
unto men, but unto God: for no man understandeth him;
howbeit in the spirit he speaketh mysteries.

1CORINTHIANS 14:2

The benefits of speaking in tongues are numerous;

This includes being able to speak to God privately
in a language no one understands.

Since the Holy Spirit is the one giving you the words
you are speaking, you are able to pray rightly and
according to God's will.

You actually edify and build up yourself as you
speak in tongues and you deal with mysteries. This
is the secret of maintaining a fresh anointing!

If you are ready to receive the gift of the Holy Spirit
with the evidence of speaking in tongues, find a
quiet place where you can pray now.

Then make these confessions after me, and after you
receive begin to speak in tongues right there where
you are.

Say "Lord Jesus, I desire the infilling with the Holy
Spirit, with the evidence of speaking in tongues. I
ask for it now. I believe that I receive it now. I

declare that I have received the gift of the Holy Spirit with the evidence of speaking in tongues. Thank you father for filling me with the Holy Spirit in Jesus name.

Now begin to speak in tongues as the Spirit gives you utterance in Jesus name!

CHAPTER 12

ELIJAH WAS A MAN

Elias was a man subject to like passions as we are, and he prayed earnestly that it might not rain: and it rained not on the earth by the space of three years and six months.

JAMES 5:17

James opens up his conversation about prayer with a remarkable statement.

He said, **'Elijah was a man!'** He was not an angel or a superman. Elijah was a man who was subject to like passions as we are. He faced challenges like every normal man.

ELIJAH WAS A MAN

When faced with certain challenges of life, it is very easy to begin to think that you are the only one facing such situations, but God wants you to know that even Elijah as powerful as he was, faced challenges like you do today.

When you consider the things that Elijah did in his days, you may be tempted to think that he was super human or that he was from another planet!

Elijah was a man with frail constitution, fears, and worries. He faced temptations, similar to what most men face today. This same Elijah called down fire from heaven and raised the son of the widow of Zarephath from the dead.

What was the secret to Elijah's life? Elijah was a man of prayer. He knew how to stay in prayer for long until supernatural manifestations begins to come.

James tells us that although Elijah was a man of like passions like we are, yet he prayed earnestly that there should be no rain in the earth for a space of three years and six months and it did not rain.

Elijah prayed again and the heavens gave rain. Prayer elevated Elijah into a class of life, higher than the normal life known to many.

James said, the effectual fervent prayer of a righteous man availeth much. The Amplified Translation says; *"The earnest (heartfelt, continued) prayer of a righteous man makes tremendous power available [dynamic in its working]."*

Elijah became tremendously powerful because he prayed earnestly. He did not just pray for a few minutes a day, he prayed continuously.

I want you to notice that there is a continuity required if we are going to see tremendous power from prayer.

Praying in the Spirit continuously for long periods of time is the secret to living a life of power.

I would like to encourage you again to give yourself to praying in tongues. As you do, you will rise above your challenges. Praying in tongues will cause you to rise above your limitations.

Prayer lifted Elijah's life above the normal human level. King Ahab was so afraid of him in his days.

ELIJAH WAS A MAN

The prophets of Baal were all destroyed when Elijah was in that flow of power and prayer.

Prayer will make you powerful like it did to Elijah. A prayer-less Christian is a powerless Christian.

I encourage you to pray in tongues a lot because it is the one way through which you can pray all day long without being tired or running short of words.

CHAPTER 13

PRAYING ON THE GO

Luke 3: 21 Now when all the people were baptized, it came to pass, that Jesus also being baptized, and praying, the heaven was opened,

LUKE 3:21

The scripture admonishes us to pray without ceasing and the secret to being able to pray without ceasing is carrying your prayer life with you on the go, throughout the day.

The scripture reveals to us that our Lord Jesus practiced praying on the go. While He was being baptised He was praying.

PRAYING ON THE GO

Our Lord Jesus was not the only one being baptised that day, however He was the only one who practiced praying at all times and it resulted in the heaven being opened and the Holy Spirit descending upon Him while He was being baptised.

When you pray on the go the anointing of the Holy Spirit will be upon you all the time. Some people find themselves only occasionally under the anointing of the Holy Spirit because they only pray occasionally.

Praying in tongues always at every time and place you find yourself causes you to be under a constant anointing of the Spirit of God.

What is praying on the go? It implies praying at all times; while you are on the road, in the car, in your office while you are sitting on your desk you can pray on the go.

To pray on the go, the best way to achieve this is by praying in tongues. Since when you pray in tongues you are not speaking to men but to God, you can actually pray in tongues at all times during every given day.

While you are cooking in the kitchen, or sitting in a saloon you can be praying in tongues. While driving in the car or sitting in a taxi you can be praying in tongues.

When you practice praying on the go like this you will discover that before the end of the day you will have accumulated a lot of hours of prayer.

There are many things that compete with our time such that we do not have enough time to pray as we ought to.

However, if you pray on the go you can actually redeem a lot of time. Paul actually admonished us in Ephesians 5 to redeem the time.

See then that ye walk circumspectly, not as fools, but as wise,

Redeeming the time, because the days are evil.

Ephesians 5:15-16

It is wisdom to learn to pray on the go as by so doing you would redeem a lot of time which ordinarily would have been lost in between other activities.

We all have only 24 hours every day and there are things which we must do to function in our different vocations.

If we will obey the bible injunction to us to pray without ceasing, we may never be able to do so by locking up ourselves in a room for 24 hours to pray, because we have other things we must attend to during the course of the day. However you can save a lot of time by praying in tongues while you do those things.

Our Lord Jesus prayed while he was being baptised showing us an example that we can actually pray while we are engaged in activities where we can multitask our prayer lives over it.

Do a time analysis right from when you wake up and start early praying on the go.

CHAPTER 14

BEING IN THE SPIRIT

I was in the Spirit on the Lord's day, and heard behind
me a great voice, as of a trumpet,

REVELATIONS 1:10

One of the amazing benefits of praying in tongues is
that when you pray in tongues you literarily move
into the realm of the spirit where revelations and
supernatural manifestations comes from.

John declared that He was in the spirit on the Lord's
day, Alleluia. What did he mean by being in the
spirit?

1 Corinthians 14:2 tells us that the way to get into
the spirit is by praying in tongues.

The gift of speaking in tongues is not an ordinary gift. It was given to us as a means for us to be able to visit the spirit world.

When you pray in tongues for long enough time, your human spirit is literarily transported into the glory world where you can hear and see things so supernatural and some of them too Holy to be uttered in the natural.

Paul spoke about how He was caught up into the third heavens and heard words which are not lawful for men to utter. How did Paul climb into that realm of the spirit?

The secret is found in what Paul said to the Corinthians.

I thank God that I speak in [strange] tongues (languages)
more than any of you or all of you put together;
Amplified Translation

1CORINTHIANS 14:18

Paul prayed in tongues a lot and he said he spoke in tongues more than the whole church of Corinth put together.

People who pray in tongues a lot, find themselves being caught up into the spirit realm of glory.

When you read the book of revelation you will think that the revelations just came to John while he was sleeping. John was in the spirit, praying in tongues when he received the revelations.

Praying in tongues for long hours opens up the spiritual realm to you that sometimes you may either be transported into that realm or angels from that realm may be authorised to come to you in the natural.

Jesus had that experience, while he was praying in Luke 9 Moses and Elijah appeared to him in the glory realm.

On another occasion angels came and strengthened Him after He had prayed.

One reason why our generation has not been seeing such supernatural flow of revelations as we ought to is because we do not know this art of being in the spirit.

I am talking about being so lost in God's presence in prayer that time becomes completely irrelevant.

God is calling us into the deep places of the Spirit and the way to get in there is by praying in tongues.

In this type of prayer, you are not praying because you have problems but rather you are praying because your heart yearns for the manifestation of the glory of heaven in your life.

You want so much of God that you devote so much time praying in tongues and fellowshipping with Him.

The Spirit of God is calling you into spending more time with Him. He is saying come up hither, come up hither into the realm of glory.

The way to answer is to begin to give yourself to praying in tongues deeply.

CHAPTER 15

THE SECRET TO PAUL'S SUCCESS

I thank God that I speak in [strange] tongues (languages)
more than any of you or all of you put together;
Amplified Translation

ICORINTHIANS 14:18

Have you ever thought about the secret to Paul's success as an Apostle?

How did Paul receive the revelation of about two thirds of the New Testament?

The secret is revealed in this declaration which Paul made about His prayer life. He said, **'I thank God that I speak in tongues more than each individual in**

the church of Corinth and more than all the church members prayer time put together.'

Paul prayed a lot in tongues. Imagine adding up all the 'praying in tongues' time of each member of the Corinthian Church and Paul's prayer exceeded them all.

That was how he gained uncommon access into the wisdom of God that enabled him to write the epistles of the New Testament.

When you speak in tongues you actually speak mysteries.

1Corinthians 14:2 tells us that in the spirit realm we speak forth mysteries when we speak in tongues.

But we speak the wisdom of God in a mystery, even the hidden wisdom, which God ordained before the world unto our glory:

1CORINTHIANS 2:7

Paul revealed to us that when we speak in tongues we are actually speaking forth the wisdom of God in a mystery.

This was how Paul gained access into divine revelations.

Paul also revealed that speaking in tongues was the secret to the anointing he walked in when he spoke about we being continuously filled with the Holy Spirit by speaking to ourselves in psalms, hymns and Spiritual songs.

Praying in tongues causes the anointing of the Spirit to rise from your human spirit upon your flesh.

No wonder the scripture declares in Acts 19:12 that Handkerchiefs and Aprons were taken from the body of Paul to the sick and the sick were healed.

Through praying in tongues Paul operated under such a unique anointing that even a venomous beast (a snake) that fastened itself on Paul's hands died instantly when it touched the anointing on Paul's hands in Acts 28:3-4

I encourage you to tap into the amazing benefits of praying in tongues and connect to God's wisdom and His Anointing in a new way.

CHAPTER 16

RESPONDING TO SATAN'S THREATS

And when they had prayed, the place was shaken where they were assembled together; and they were all filled with the Holy Ghost, and they spake the word of God with boldness.

ACTS 4:31

When the Apostles were threatened by the elders of Israel, they did not take their threats as empty threats because these people who threatened them were the same people who crucified Jesus.

The scripture reveals that the Apostles responded to the threats they faced by giving themselves to prayer.

Today, there are many things threatening the peace and prosperity of believers, God wants us to respond the right way by giving ourselves to prayer.

After the Apostles had prayed, the place where they were assembled was shaken by the power of the Holy Spirit. There is a shaking that God has promised to bring in the book of Haggai in the last days.

This shaking comes when believers begin to respond to the activities of Satan by rising up in prayer. Praying in the spirit until the power of the Holy Ghost falls and shakes up the environment.

Are you facing threats in any aspect of your life? Are you facing financial difficulties? Do not spend your time crying or mourning. Rise up and pray.

Prayer makes you unstoppable. The scripture declares that the Apostles were filled with the Holy Ghost and spoke the word of God with boldness.

RESPONDING TO SATAN'S THREATS

We need a new baptism of the Spirit of boldness in our lives today. The secret to this is praying in the spirit.

When you pray in tongues you build up yourself on your most Holy Faith. Praying in tongues makes you to walk in an uncommon anointing of boldness like you may never have walked in before.

I encourage you to rise up and let your prayer steam go up to heaven.

> And now, Lord, behold their threatenings: and grant unto thy servants, that with all boldness they may speak thy word,
>
> By stretching forth thine hand to heal; and that signs and wonders may be done by the name of thy holy child Jesus.
>
> Acts 4:29-30

If you examine the prayers the Apostles prayed when they were threatened, you will notice that they did not go to God in fear or anguish of soul. Rather they outlined their requests based carefully.

Firstly they asked for boldness. They asked for boldness because they knew their authority in Christ and that no threat from hell could stop them as long as they did not become timid.

It is important to state that every born again Christian has been elevated into a position of authority such that no threat from the devil can actually hurt you as long as you do not become timid.

If there is anything we need today, I believe it is the spirit of might and boldness.

Secondly, they asked God to stretch forth His hands to do signs and wonders.

I believe that God wants us to make these same requests today as we spend time in prayers.

CHAPTER 17

PROMOTING YOUR GROWTH IN WISDOM GRACE AND BLESSEDNESS

1 Corinthians 14: 4 He that speaketh in an unknown tongue edifieth himself; but he that prophesieth edifieth the church.

1CORINTHIANS 14:4

He who makes use of the gift of speaking in tongues does good to himself, builds himself up and promotes his own spiritual growth.

The Greek word translated edify in 1Corinthians 14:4 is the word oikodemeo; which means to build a house or to erect a building.

The scripture describes us as the New Testament house of God. God has chosen to dwell in us. Through His Holy Spirit He has come to live in us.

By using the gift of speaking in tongues, we build up ourselves and we grow up into a Holy Temple where the fullness of the Holy Spirit's presence can manifest. The manifestation of the Holy Spirit in our lives is what causes us to profit.

Do you feel sometimes spiritually dry? The reason is because you do not speak in tongues at all or you do not do so enough.

God wants to manifest His presence in your life but you need to build up yourself a Holy Temple unto Him through praying in tongues.

There are degrees of the manifestation of the presence of God. God's manifest presence in your life is only to the extent to which you have built up yourself.

You promote your own spiritual growth into a Holy Temple in the lord by praying in tongues.

PROMOTING YOUR GROWTH IN WISDOM, GRACE AND BLESSEDNESS

The word 'edify' also means to promote your own spiritual growth in wisdom, grace and blessedness.

When you pray in tongues, you speak forth the wisdom of God in a mystery, which wisdom manifests at every time of need. That is why people who pray in tongues a lot are always full of wisdom. Stephen was a classic example of a New Testament man who was full of wisdom.

Stephen was full of the Holy Ghost and wisdom because he prayed in tongues a lot.

The scripture reveals to us that the Jews could not resist the wisdom by which he spoke in Acts 6:10. We know Stephen got this wisdom by praying in tongues because he was full of the Holy Ghost and you become full of the Holy Ghost by praying in tongues.

Paul prayed in tongues more than the whole Church of Corinth put together and the Apostle Peter in 2 Peter 3:15 described Paul as one who was given uncommon wisdom. Paul got this wisdom by praying in tongues.

When you pray in tongues you promote your own growth in grace. When you pray in tongues, you commune with the Holy Spirit and you activate the following scripture;

The grace of the Lord Jesus Christ, and the love of God, and the communion of the Holy Ghost, be with you all. Amen.

2Corinthians 13:14

The grace of the Lord Jesus Christ, the love of God and all spiritual forces are communicated to us through communion with the Holy Spirit. You commune with the Holy Spirit through praying in tongues.

When you pray in tongues you promote your own spiritual growth in the blessing of Abraham. This is what it means when the scripture says he who prays in tongues edifies himself.

CHAPTER 18

CONNECTING TO DEEPER MEASURES OF GRACE

2Corinthians 13:14 The grace of the Lord Jesus Christ, and the love of God, and the communion of the Holy Ghost, be with you all. Amen.

2CORINTHIANS 13:14

The grace of the Lord Jesus Christ, the love of God and all good spiritual forces are communicated into your life through communion with the Holy Spirit. When you pray in tongues you commune with the Holy Spirit.

The Holy Spirit holds the key to grace. Grace is God's divine favours which causes you to possess your inheritance without struggles.

In Genesis 6:8, Noah enjoyed God's divine grace and favour in such a way that God revealed His plan to destroy the world to Noah and instructed him to build an ark. Noah actually received what we call in the New Testament, the gift of Word of Wisdom as God revealed His plan for the future to Him.

This shows us one reason why when we pray in tongues, God reveals things to us. When you pray in tongues, the grace of God is communicated to you and such grace and favour of God brings revelations to you just like Noah received revelations because he found grace in God's sight.

Through praying in tongues, you can gain access to all the other gifts of the Holy Spirit as listed in 1Corinthians 12 because these gifts of the Spirit are acts of God's grace and praying in tongues unleashes the rivers of grace upon you.

We can better understand what was happening in Acts 19: 6 as a result of this light.

And when Paul had laid his hands upon the twelve disciples in Ephesus, the Holy Ghost came on them; and they spake with tongues, and prophesied.

Why did prophesying accompany the disciples after speaking in tongues? When Paul laid his hands on them, they spoke with tongues and connected to grace.

According to Romans 12:6, we receive different gifts according to the grace that is given to us.

So they received the gift of prophecy because the grace for the gift of prophecy was made available to them as they communed with the Holy Spirit through praying in tongues.

A deeper measure of grace is communicated to us when we pray in tongues.

The gift of speaking in tongues itself is a fruit of the grace for salvation. This is so because our Lord Jesus said that everyone who believes on Him will be saved, and speak in tongues as a sign. That is why every saved believer should speak in tongues.

When we speak in tongues we commune with the Holy Spirit and greater measures of grace is poured out upon us resulting in acts of God's favour seen in our lives.

Do you need grace in any aspect of your life? I encourage you to give yourself to praying in tongues.

CHAPTER 19

ENTERING GOD'S REST

For with stammering lips and another tongue will he speak to this people.

To whom he said, This is the rest wherewith ye may cause the weary to rest; and this is the refreshing: yet they would not hear.

ISAIAH 28:11-12

God has provided a cure for all forms of fatigue. It is amazing to discover how much praying in tongues helps your physical body to rest and be refreshed. Praying in tongues also ignites your human Spirit with the flames of glory, while energising your mind and helps it to rest.

The word from the lips of God the father Himself is worth making note of. 'This is the rest wherewith ye may cause the weary to rest', God said. This is the authentic, heaven sanctioned mode of rest given by heaven. With stammering lips and another tongue will he speak to this people.

There is a part of this prophecy of Isaiah about speaking in tongues that is a warning. He said, 'yet they would not hear.' Implying that many people would not pay attention to God's provision for rest revealed in His word.

Let us not be among those who would not hear. Let us hearken to the voice of the Holy Spirit by dedicating ourselves to praying always in the spirit. The emphasis is on praying always, without ceasing in the spirit.

Speaking in tongues is the way to spiritual rest. Times of refreshing comes to you when you dedicate yourself to praying in tongues.

Are you weary? Do you feel fatigued? Do you need spiritual and physical refreshing? God has provided a way to rest and be refreshed. Speak in tongues. Spend quality time praying in tongues and you will be refreshed.

He who speaks in tongues edifies or refreshes himself.

In Hebrews 4: 9 the scripture declares, *"There remaineth therefore a rest to the people of God."*

This is called the reserved rest for the righteous. God does not want righteous people struggling. He has reserved a rest for us. What is this rest? It speaks of a life free from struggles. How do we enter into it? We must believe in God's provision for rest. What is the secret of enjoying God's provision for rest? Speaking in tongues! He said this is the rest.

The children of Israel did not enter into their rest because of unbelief. We who believe what God said about speaking in tongues and give ourselves to speaking in tongues, do enter into God's rest.

Some may say but I do not believe everybody should speak in tongues. Well, if you are in unbelief, then you cannot enter into God's rest through unbelief.

Let us labour therefore to enter into that rest, lest any man fall after the same example of unbelief.

HEBREWS 4:11

Did you know that praying in tongues is the way to enter into God's rest? I motivate you today, begin to labour to enter into that rest by labouring in prayer. Pray into tongues until you find rest on every side.

Financial rest awaits you. No more struggles financially. Pray in tongues and enter into financial rest.

CHAPTER 20

INVOKING THE BLESSING

What is it then? I will pray with the spirit, and I
will pray with the understanding also: I will sing
with the spirit, and I will sing with the
understanding also.

Else when thou shalt bless with the spirit, how
shall he that occupieth the room of the unlearned
say Amen at thy giving of thanks, seeing he
understandeth not what thou sayest?

1CORINTHIANS 14:15-16

When the children of Israel were going into the land
of Canaan, God gave them the blessing and
commanded them to apply it to the land when they
get there.

Behold, I set before you this day a blessing and a curse;

DEUTERONOMY 11:26

They were to put this blessing or the curse upon the land.

And it shall come to pass, when the LORD thy God hath brought thee in unto the land whither thou goest to possess it, that thou shalt put the blessing upon mount Gerizim, and the curse upon mount Ebal.

DEUTERONOMY 11:29

In Christ Jesus God has given us the blessing according to Ephesians 1:3. This blessing is in the spirit realm.

It is important to understand that the blessings with which our Lord Jesus blessed us are all spiritual and are located in the spirit realm in the anointing.

We must learn how to bring these blessings into practical use on an everyday basis. In the Old Testament God told them to put the blessing upon their land.

To us that means learning to put the blessing on our marriage, health, finances etc.

God did not only give us the blessing, He has also given us a way to sprinkle the blessing upon every aspect of our lives by giving us the gift of speaking in tongues.

Paul said in 1Corinthians 14:16 *'Else when thou shall bless with the spirit'* referring to the fact that through praying in tongues, we actually take up the blessing and sprinkle it upon any area of need in our lives.

The Greek word translated *'Bless'* in that scripture is the word *'eulogeo'* and it means *'to invoke the blessing',* among other things.

When you speak in tongues, you invoke the bless into operation. You take it up as a spiritual substance and you apply it on every area of need in your life.

We are already blessed in Christ Jesus. However, many Christians are still suffering as though they are under the curse.

Some Christians are even going from one place to another trying to break the curse which Christ has already broken many years ago simply because they do not know how to reach into the spirit realm to take up the blessing and put it upon their lives.

When you speak in tongues, you actually enter into the realm of the spirit where your blessings reside and you bring them down into all aspects of your life for practical use.

Today we have that responsibility to reach into the spirit realm and take up the blessing and sprinkle it upon every aspect of our lives.

I encourage you to speak in tongues and invoke the blessing into your areas of need

.

CHAPTER 21

MAINTAINING A PRAYERFUL LIFE

And he withdrew himself into the wilderness, and prayed.

LUKE 5:16

We can learn the secrets to maintaining a prayerful life by examining the prayer life of our Lord Jesus Christ. The scripture records that He practiced withdrawal.

In Luke 5:15, the scripture records that Jesus became very busy and famous in such a way that great multitudes came to hear Him, and to be healed.

In the midst of His busy schedule, Jesus pulled Himself apart and went into a wilderness and prayed.

As God blesses you, you will become very busy in such a way that you may find yourself being choked physically with activities; however you need to learn to withdraw into prayer like Jesus did.

We also noticed that one of the secrets of our Lord Jesus' successful prayer life is revealed in the following scripture.

And in the morning, rising up a great while before day, he went out, and departed into a solitary place, and there prayed.

MARK 1:35

Firstly, our Lord Jesus prayed early in the morning. When you pray in the morning you start your day right. Secondly, our Lord Jesus rose up from where He slept and went out to a solitary place. Many people wake up but stay on their bed while trying to pray. The danger in that is that you could fall asleep again while lying on your bed.

When you wake up, get up from the bed and find a quiet place where you can pray. It could simply mean going from your bed room to your sitting room or going into your garage if you have any. The key factor is getting up. The act of getting up in the morning wakes you up.

Also when you set out to pray, make sure you actually pray. Some people set out to pray and end up being distracted. Beware of distractions. The devil uses distractions of different kinds to stop many from praying.

A relationship sometimes can be a huge distraction especially if you are in a relationship with someone who does not have desire for the things of God. That person will always draw you back spiritually.

Another secret to maintaining a good prayer life is recognising the fact that praying is a very important key to your all round success and any day that goes without you praying always turns out different.

Surround yourself with prayerful people. If you are surrounded with people who pray, their prayer life will motivate you.

And it came to pass, that, as he was praying in a certain place, when he ceased, one of his disciples said unto him, Lord, teach us to pray, as John also taught his disciples.

LUKE 11:1

The disciples of Jesus were motivated to want to pray because they saw him praying. If you surround yourself with people who are do not pray, you will find yourself losing the desire for prayer.

CHAPTER 22

SECRET PLACE DWELLERS

Psalms 91:1 He that dwelleth in the secret place of the most High shall abide under the shadow of the Almighty.

PSALMS 91:1

In the Old Testament, the secret place of the most high speaks about the Holy of Holies in the tabernacle.

The Holy of Holies is the place of intimate worship and fellowship with God the father. Inside there, all you will find is the sweet incense of worship of Israel, the table of shewbread, the Ark of the Covenant containing the Ten Commandments and only the High Priest was permitted to go in there.

God promised to meet Israel inside this Holy of Holies and to speak with them there in Exodus 25:22

To us today the secret place of the most high speaks about the time you set aside to be with God alone. Alone with God, in prayer and spirit worship.

The father is seeking for secret place dwellers. He is seeking for Spirit Worship. He is seeking for men and women who will dedicate a lot of time to praying in tongues.

We worship in spirit by praying in tongues. He who speaks in tongues speaks to God in the spirit and shares intimacies just between him and God.

There are amazing benefits of being a secret place dweller. A secret place dweller is one who prays all the time. He does not just observe his quiet time; rather he learns to pray in tongues throughout the day.

He that dwells in the secret place of the most high shall abide under the shadows of the almighty. When you pray in tongues all the time you become literarily clothed with the Shekinah glory of God.

SECRET PLACE DWELLERS

When you pray in tongues all the time, God delivers you from the snare of the fowler and from the noisome pestilence.

When you pray in tongues, God covers you with his feathers and under his wings you will trust.

When you pray in tongues, you will not be afraid of the terror by night nor of the arrow that flies by day.

When you pray in tongues, you will not be afraid of the pestilence that walketh in darkness and you will not fear the destruction that wasteth at noonday.

No evil shall befall you neither shall any plague come near the dwelling of secret place dwellers.

God gives His angels charge over the lives of secret place dwellers and they keep them in all their ways.

Praying in tongues opens you up to the ministry of angels. In Matthew 4:11, after Jesus had finished praying, angels came and ministered to him.

I motivate you today to become a secret place dweller. Carry your prayer life with you on the go. Pray in the spirit until you can pray no more and pray some more

CHAPTER 23

THE GENERATION THAT SEEKS HIS FACE

Who shall ascend into the hill of the LORD? or who shall stand in his holy place?

He that hath clean hands, and a pure heart; who hath not lifted up his soul unto vanity, nor sworn deceitfully.

He shall receive the blessing from the LORD, and righteousness from the God of his salvation.

This is the generation of them that seek him, that seek thy face, O Jacob. Selah.

PSALM 24:3-6

THE GENERATION THAT SEEKS HIS FACE

I would like to motivate you to become a part of a different generation. A generation of people who ascend to the hill of God and who stand in His Holy place.

A generation of people who worship Him in spirit and in truth. Our Lord Jesus said that the father is seeking for such to worship him.

What makes a man to spend a lot of time in prayer? The first key is having a hunger for God, to know Him more and to be a carrier of His manifest presence.

Spiritual hunger is what drives prayer. If you are satisfied with your spiritual life and you are content with where you are in your walk with God you will not see the need to spend time with God in prayer.

Your prayer life will only be as deep as the depth of your hunger for God's manifest presence. God is everywhere but the reality of God's manifest presence is not everywhere.

The psalmist said that those who will ascend to God's hill and stand in His presence in prayer are simply people who seek through spiritual hunger the Glory that shines from the face of Jesus.

The generation of those who seek God's face speaks about the people who spend time to fellowship with God in prayer to hear His voice, to be guided by His eyes and just to bask in the beauty of His presence.

The people in this class are described as people who have clean hands and pure hearts.

Sin is one of the things that destroy your prayer life. Once you practice sinning and you live in it every day or make excuses for your sinful behaviour instead of honestly repenting and making effort to stop such actions, your prayer life will die off.

Sin breaks your fellowship with God but genuine and honest repentance will bring you back on track.

If you are in any sinful situation now, I encourage you to come out of such. Quit any relationship that makes you commit the sin of fornication and adultery.

Abstain from all appearances of evil and the very God of peace will sanctify you wholly.

And I pray God that your whole spirit and soul and body will be preserved blameless unto the coming of the lord in Jesus mighty name.

CHAPTER 24

SPIRITUAL INITIATIVE IN THE PRAYER OF SUPPLICATION

Do not fret or have any anxiety about anything, but in every circumstance and in everything, by prayer and petition (definite requests), with thanksgiving, continue to make your wants known to God. Amplified Translation

PHILIPPIANS 4:6

The prayer of supplication is one of the scriptural types of prayer that God wants us to pray. Most people approach God with their supplications and many times do not receive because they lack the

New Testament spiritual understanding of the right approach to the prayer of supplication.

When you come to God with your needs, you do not come lamenting or crying about how terrible things are and so on. Paul said do not fret. Do not come in anxiety and that is a command you must obey if you want answers.

The Greek word translated supplication is the word 'deeiss' and the Thayers dictionary of Greek words defines that word as a need or want in your life.

It also defines that word as the act of seeking, asking or making request to God about the need or want.

That word is translated sometimes as petition, request or supplication.

God expects us to present our requests before him through our high priest who is in heaven for us as our advocate.

When you pray, It is important for you to have a scriptural basis for your prayer and you should quote the promise God made to Him, putting Him in remembrance of His promise to you in that area.

SPIRITUAL INITIATIVE IN THE PRAYER OF SUPPLICATION

Remind Him about what He promised you on the basis of which you make such request.

It is not that God forgot that He made such promises, however He said in the following scripture;

> Put me in remembrance: let us plead together: declare thou, that thou mayest be justified.

ISAIAH 43:6

Taking God's word and telling Him in prayer what He said and that you believe it, is an act of praying in faith.

So God asked us to put Him in remembrance of what He promised us as a demonstration of our faith, both in God and in what God said.

A prayer of petition can simply be you asking for mercy on the grounds of what our Lord Jesus' already did for a situation to be turned around.

You should say, 'father, Jesus was wounded and with His stripes I was healed. Therefore 'I request the manifestation of the healing in my body bringing forth my healing and glory to your name'.

Your prayer could be you seeking favour from God over a matter.

If it is mercy you need, you can quote Hebrews 4:16; which says we should come boldly to the throne of grace to obtain mercy and favour to help in time of need.

A key factor in the prayer of supplication or petition is that you should ask and continue to make your wants known with thanksgiving.

Never come to God in mourning and sorrow, telling Him how horrible things are. Rather take God's word and tell Him what He said and do it with praise and thanksgiving for the performance of His word.

CHAPTER 25

THE WILL OF GOD AND THE PRAYER OF SUPPLICATION

And this is the confidence that we have in him, that, if we ask any thing according to his will, he heareth us:

And if we know that he hear us, whatsoever we ask, we know that we have the petitions that we desired of him.

1JOHN 5:14-15

A significant requirement to receiving answers to the prayer of supplication is asking according to the will of God.

John said that our foundation for faith or confidence when we pray is hinged on knowing the will of God.

If you pray, faith is the basis upon which God answers your prayers. You cannot have faith if you are not sure whether what you are praying about is the will of God or not.

If you do not have confidence that God will hear you when you pray, you cannot receive what you asked for.

You will only receive the petitions you ask for if you are confident that God hears you and that confidence cannot exist if you are unsure whether it is God's will or if you pray whereas you know that it is not God's will.

A common mistake many Christians make is that they think God will answer just anything they ask for, simply because our Lord Jesus said in *Matthew 7:8 that every one that asketh receiveth; and those who seek find; and to him that knocketh the door shall be opened.*

God does not answer us every time we pray just because we prayed; rather He answers only when we pray in faith according to His will in the situation.

Now someone may say, 'but how do I know whether it is the will of God for me to receive a particular thing?'

The answer is very simple. God has revealed His will to you in the bible. Once you have a scriptural promise you can base your faith on, then you can pray with confidence.

If you are praying for a life partner for example, and you are already in love with someone; If you go to God to ask Him to make the person concerned propose to you, you may be praying amiss because even though God promised to give you a life partner, He never told you that, that specific individual is the person.

Situations have arisen where a girl feels that God has spoken to her that a particular guy is her life partner whereas the guy in question does not feel the same as the girl does (This also happens the other way round).

It is always safer when you pray for such things to always ask God for His will be done and not necessarily your desires because your desires may just be based on lust.

When your petitions are made and you are not clear whether it is the will of God for you to receive such petition or not, it is always very important to simply ask God to fulfil His purpose in the situation rather than trying to force God to make your desires become His will.

You cannot force God to make your desires become His will. You may force your way and go ahead with what you want to do and God may not stop you but that does not imply that you are in the center of God's will in the situation.

Living in the center of God's will is the secret to prosperity.

CHAPTER 26

CONFESSION; GIVING VOICE TO GOD'S WORD

Whosoever therefore shall confess me before men, him will I confess also before my Father which is in heaven.

MATTHEW 10:32

Our Lord Jesus Christ revealed an amazing fact about his present day ministry for us before the father in this statement in Matthew 10:32

Every time we take God's word and begin to confess it on the earth. Every time we speak to the hearing of people and our words are filled with God's word; our Lord Jesus sees it as we confessing Him before men and in turn He goes before the father as your

SHARING INTIMACIES WITH GOD

High Priest and acknowledges you and all you affirm before the father.

> In the beginning was the Word, and the Word was with God, and the Word was God.

> JOHN 1:1

The scriptures describe Our Lord Jesus as the Word of God. As the Word of God, He is the expression of God the father to us.

When God the father through His Holy Spirit speaks, He reveals Jesus. This is what Our Lord Jesus meant when He said the Holy Spirit when he comes will testify of Him or will admit to everything that Jesus is, has done and has obtained.

> But when the Comforter is come, whom I will send unto you from the Father, even the Spirit of truth, which proceedeth from the Father, he shall testify of me:

> JOHN 15:26

The Holy Spirit is God the father dwelling with in us today and every time He speaks He actually reveals Jesus who is the word of the father to us.

Our Lord Jesus said, 'if you confess me, I will confess you before God in heaven.'

What does it mean to confess Jesus? To confess Him means to confess the words of God. Our Lord Jesus is the word of God.

Every word written in the bible that gives expression to the promises of God, who God is, what Jesus has done for us, who we are in Christ Jesus, what we have in Christ Jesus and what we can do in Christ Jesus MUST become our confession.

Confession is a form of prayer. Hebrews describes Jesus as the high priest over our confession. Indicating that our Lord Jesus takes up every confession we make on earth and brings it before the father.

Also I say unto you, Whosoever shall confess me before men, him shall the Son of man also confess before the angels of God:

LUKE 12:8

In Luke's rendering of this account it tells us that when we confess God's word in the earth before men, Jesus takes your confession to the father, gets authorisation for what you confessed to be implemented from the father and then He authorises your angels to carry out what you confessed. This is an important spiritual cycle of how to get things from the realm of the spirit.

CHAPTER 27

HOW TO ENSURE THAT YOUR PRAYERS ARE ANSWERED

James 4:1 From whence come wars and fightings among you? come they not hence, even of your lusts that war in your members?

2 Ye lust, and have not: ye kill, and desire to have, and cannot obtain: ye fight and war, yet ye have not, because ye ask not.

3 Ye ask, and receive not, because ye ask amiss, that ye may consume it upon your lusts.

JAMES 4:1-3

One reason why may people do not have the things they desire is because they do not ask.

They complain about their problems, they cry about how busy the devil is but they do not come to God with a specific request or petition of what they want God to do.

It is important for you to learn to specifically ask for what you desire.

Secondly, when you ask, you must not ask for what heaven has already forbidden you from having.

James said, you ask and receive not because you ask amiss. Many prayer requests are a mistake submitted to heaven hence our lord high priest, Jesus Christ does not process it.

The core mistake that most people make for which reason they do not receive answers to their prayers is that they ask for things that heaven has not permitted for them to have.

James puts it this way, he said 'You ask, and receive not, because you ask amiss, that ye may consume it upon your lusts.'

HOW TO ENSURE THAT YOUR PRAYERS ARE ANSWERED

Lust is simply desiring anything forbidden. Lust means, wanting to have something that the bible has already told you that it is not the will of God for you to have.

An example would be, being in a relationship with someone who is not born again and then praying for God to make the relationship with such a person to work out.

God already forbids you from being yoked in relationship with an unbeliever in 2Corinthians 6:14

James said such lust cannot be granted no matter how many times you cry to God in prayer.

The rule for what you should ask for is outlined in the following scripture;

Truly I tell you, whatever you forbid and declare to be improper and unlawful on earth must be what is already forbidden in heaven, and whatever you permit and declare proper and lawful on earth must be what is already permitted in heaven. AMPLIFIED TRANSLATION

MATTHEW 18:18

What you ask God to do on earth should be what heaven has already approved for you to have on earth.

You cannot just make any request and expect God to answer it. God only grants on earth what He has approved or permitted for you to have in heaven.

It is therefore important to first try to establish whether it is the will of God for you to have what you are asking God before you start asking.

God may not stop you from walking in disobedience outside His will especially when you are stubborn and want to proceed to have your lusts but you will not find joy or peace when you take such steps because you are outside of the will of God.

CHAPTER 28

FORGIVENESS AND THE PRAYER OF SUPPLICATION

And when you assume the posture of prayer, remember
that it's not all asking . If you have anything against
someone, forgive —only then will your heavenly Father
be inclined to also wipe your slate clean of sins."
Message Translation

MARK 11:25

The message translation of Mark 11:25 shows us
that when praying the prayer of supplication, it is
not only all about asking in prayers that gets the job
done.

There are other factors that affect receiving answers
to prayers. One of them is forgiveness. When you

stand praying and you have something in your mind against someone, you must forgive them.

Unforgiveness stops your prayers from being answered. There are many Christians who have been wondering why it seems like their prayers are not being answered. If you are in that space, you need to examine your life to see if there is someone who hurt you who you have not forgiven.

Some have determined never to forgive or have anything to do with certain people in their lives because of what they did to them. I would like you to know that if you refuse to forgive; such unforgiveness will hinder all your prayers from being answered.

Give forgiveness as a free gift, do not wait for people to merit your forgiveness before you give it. It controls receiving answers to prayers.

And forgive us our debts, as we forgive our debtors.

For if ye forgive men their trespasses, your heavenly Father will also forgive you:

But if ye forgive not men their trespasses, neither will your Father forgive your trespasses.

MATTHEW 6:12-15

FORGIVENESS AND THE PRAYER OF SUPPLICATION

God measures out forgiveness to you using the same scale with which you measure forgiveness to people.

Forgiving people is not for their sakes but for your sake. Most times people may not deserve for you to forgive them. However, if you think about the fact that not forgiving them will negatively affect your prayers according to the scripture, then you must choose to forgive them.

I encourage you to be slow to anger and quick to forgive when you are hurt. Do not hold grudges against anyone.

If there is someone who hurt you, go to such a person now and offer them forgiveness. Tell them that you have forgiven them. God forgave the world and sent us to go and preach forgiveness of sins so the sinners can know that they are forgiven.

Act like God today!

I declare grace upon you now to forgive anyone who may have hurt you badly in Jesus name.

About the Author

Emmanuel Ogbechie is the president of Divine Representatives Ministries Inc and Senior Pastor of Diplomats Assembly Churches.

He is also the president of In His Presence Bible School with learning centres in South Africa, Nigeria and Kenya

He is the host of In His Presence Radio and TV broadcast.

A graduate of Electrical and Electronics Engineering, he is married to Pastor Idowu Ogbechie

OTHER BOOKS BY THE AUTHOR

PHYSICS OF MONEY

Money moves! Money was designed to move. It is either moving away from you or moving towards you.

Physics of money reveals the dynamics of the movement of money and shows you how you can harness the ever moving attribute of money.

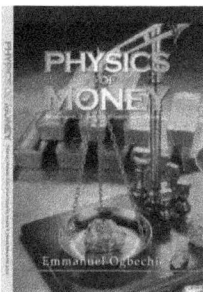

If you desire financial freedom, the physics of Money is a must read. It is written in simple and concise language and will spur into action, so that you can move from where you are to where you desire to be financially. It is financial Intelligence expose at its best.

ISBN:

9781463502423

HOW

GRACE

WORKS

A Revelation of the Dynamics of the Operation of Grace

by

Pastor Emmanuel Ogbechie

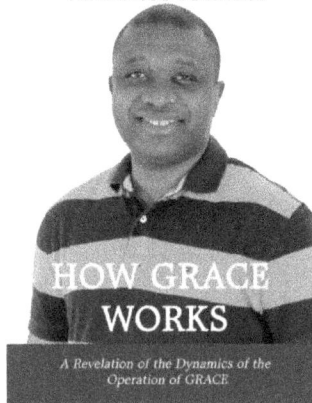

Everything God does in the New Testament He does it by Grace. God does everything He does by grace so that no one can glory in His sight that he obtained any height by his effort.

When Jesus walked the streets of Jerusalem, he lived to demonstrate to us how the grace of God works. If you do not know how grace works, you will not be able to experience its operation in your life as you desire.

In this book Pastor Emmanuel Ogbechie will help you discover HOW GRACE WORKS. You will learn about the operational procedure of the grace of God and this knowledge will catapult you to receive and experience a greater measure of the workings of God in your life.

The Law came by Moses but Jesus Christ brought the knowledge of Grace and how it works.

Pastor Emmanuel Ogbechie, host of In His Presence Radio and TV Broadcasts, is the founder and senior Pastor of Diplomats Assembly Churches also known as Divine Representatives Ministries Inc. He is the President of In His Presence Bible School and author of physics of money.

www.ingramcontent.com/pod-product-compliance
Lightning Source LLC
Chambersburg PA
CBHW051637050426
42443CB00025B/411

The Law of Attraction:

How to Get
Your Man

The Slam-Dunk Formula
to Getting the Love of Your Life

Sally Huss

Huss Publishing
www.sallyhuss.com

Huss Publishing
P.O. Box 206
La Jolla, California 90038
©2009 Sally Huss
www.sallyhuss.com
Book design by Reza Izadkhah
Edited by Janet Muniz

ISBN-10 0982262523
ISBN-13 9780982262528